CLIFTON PARK-HALFMOON PUBLIC LIBRARY

W9-AHY-640

CLIFTON PARK-HALFMOON PUBLIC LIBRARY

Nineteenth-Century Migration to America

Clifton Park - Halfmoon Public Library
475 Moe Road
Clifton Park, New York 12065

John Bliss

Raintree
Chicago, Illinois

www.heinemannraintree.com
Visit our website to find out more information about Heinemann-Raintree books.

To order:
☎ Phone 888-454-2279
💻 Visit www.heinemannraintree.com to browse our catalog and order online.

© 2012 Raintree
an imprint of Capstone Global Library, LLC
Chicago, Illinois

All rights reserved. No part of this publication may be reproduced or transmitted in any form or by any means, electronic or mechanical, including photocopying, recording, taping, or any information storage and retrieval system, without permission in writing from the publisher.

Edited by Louise Galpine, Abby Colich, and Diyan Leake
Designed by Richard Parker
Original illustrations © Capstone Global Library Ltd 2011
Illustrated by Jeff Edwards
Picture research by Mica Brancic

Originated by Capstone Global Library Ltd
Printed and bound in the United States of America,
North Mankato, MN

15 14 13 12 11
10 9 8 7 6 5 4 3 2

Library of Congress Cataloging-in-Publication Data
Bliss, John.
   Nineteenth century migration to America / John Bliss.
      p. cm.—(Children's true stories : migration)
   Includes bibliographical references and index.
   ISBN 978-1-4109-4074-2 (hardcover)—ISBN 978-1-4109-4080-3 (pbk.) 1. United States—Emigration and immigration—History—19th century—Juvenile literature. I. Title.
   JV6451.B55 2012
   304.8'73009034—dc22   2010039326

Acknowledgments
We would like to thank the following for permission to reproduce photographs: Alamy p. 21 (© Mike Booth); The Art Archive p. 13 (Free library Philadelphia); © Corbis pp. 12 (Bettmann), 17 (© Bojan Brecelj), 24 (© Photo Collection Alexander Alland, Sr./Robert L. Bracklow); East Lothian Council Museum's Service p. 7; Getty Images pp. 4 (Archive Photos/Fotosearch), 14 (Museum of the City of New York/Byron Collection), 16 (Archive Photos/Buyenlarge), 20 (FPG), 22 (De Agostini/DEA/M. Borchi), 25 (Buyenlarge), 26 (The Christian Science Monitor/Melanie Stetson Freeman); Shutterstock pp. 5 (© Iladm), 10 (© Ritu Manoj Jethani), 11 (© Kevin Swope), 19 (© Caitlin Mirra); Wisconsin Historical Society p. 9.

Cover photograph of an Italian immigrant family on board a ferry from the docks to Ellis Island, New York, 1905, reproduced with permission of Getty Images (Hulton Archive/Lewis W. Hine).

We would like to acknowledge the following sources of material: p. 10 from the Sierra Club website, "The Story of My Boyhood and Youth" by John Muir, http://www.sierraclub.org/john_muir_exhibit/frameindex.html?http://www.sierraclub.org/john_muir_exhibit/writings/the_story_of_my_boyhood_and_youth/chapter_3.html. Accessed on September 7, 2010; pp. 12–17 from "The Biography of a Chinaman," by Lee Chew, *Independent*, 15 (February 19, 1903), 417–423; pp. 22–26 from Barry Moreno, *Ellis Island's Famous Immigrant* (Charleston, S.C.: Arcadia Publishing, 2008).

We would like to thank Professor Sarah Chinn for her invaluable help in the preparation of this book.

Every effort has been made to contact copyright holders of material reproduced in this book. Any omissions will be rectified in subsequent printings if notice is given to the publisher.

Disclaimer
All the Internet addresses (URLs) given in this book were valid at the time of going to press. However, due to the dynamic nature of the Internet, some addresses may have changed, or sites may have changed or ceased to exist since publication. While the author and publisher regret any inconvenience this may cause readers, no responsibility for any such changes can be accepted by either the author or the publisher.

082011
006318RP

Contents

DAILY LIFE
Read here to learn what life was like for the children in these stories, and the impact that migrating had at home and at school.

NUMBER CRUNCHING
Find out the details about migration and the numbers of people involved.

Migrants'Lives
Read these boxes to find out what happened to the children in this book when they grew up.

HELPING HAND
Find out how people and organizations have helped children to migrate.

On the Scene
Read eyewitness accounts of migration in the migrants' own words.

Some words are printed in bold, **like this**. You can find out what they mean by looking in the glossary on page 30.

A Country of Immigrants

The United States is a country of **immigrants**. Everyone who lives there has family who once lived in another country. Even the American Indians may have come from another land. Some scientists believe they crossed into North America through what is now Alaska more than 10,000 years ago.

"The streets are paved with gold"

Between 1815 and 1914, more than 30 million people **migrated** to the United States. Some, like the Chinese, went to work on the railroads and in the mines. Irish and Jewish immigrants went because of troubles at home. All of them went to the United States looking for a new life. People had heard the streets were paved with gold. They came to get their share.

More than 100 million Americans have family members who came to the United States through the immigration station on Ellis Island, in New York.

On the scene

A poem displayed in the Statue of Liberty has these words:

Give me your tired, your poor

*Your huddled masses **yearning** to breathe free*

Many immigrants to the United States were poor people looking for a better life. They could identify with these words.

For many immigrants, the Statue of Liberty in New York was the first view of their new home.

Scotland 1849

Immigration to the United States exploded in the middle of the 1800s. By the 1850s, 2.6 million people a year were going there. Most of these people were from the United Kingdom, Germany, and Scandinavia. Many were drawn to the United States by the rich farmland of the **Midwest**.

Nature boy

John Muir was born in Dunbar, on the southeast coast of Scotland, in 1838. He fell in love with nature when he was only three. His grandfather took him on walks in the country and showed him the fruit and wildlife. He had a small plot to tend in the family garden.

One night in 1849, John's father came in with exciting news. The family was moving to the United States. John would go on ahead with his father, his older sister, and his younger brother. His mother would stay behind with the younger children until the family was settled.

DAILY LIFE

John Muir and his friends played in the ruins of Dunbar Castle, which was close to where he lived. It was more than 1,000 years old. There would be no castles for him in his new home.

John Muir grew up in this house in Scotland.

To the New World

It took six weeks to cross the ocean by ship. John's father and sister stayed below with the "old folk," but John and his brother went on deck. They watched the sailors and played with other boys.

The ship carried many **emigrants** (people who were moving from their original country) to North America. John's father had planned to settle in Canada, but when he heard about the fine soil in the state of Wisconsin, he made that their destination. Wisconsin had just become part of the United States the year before.

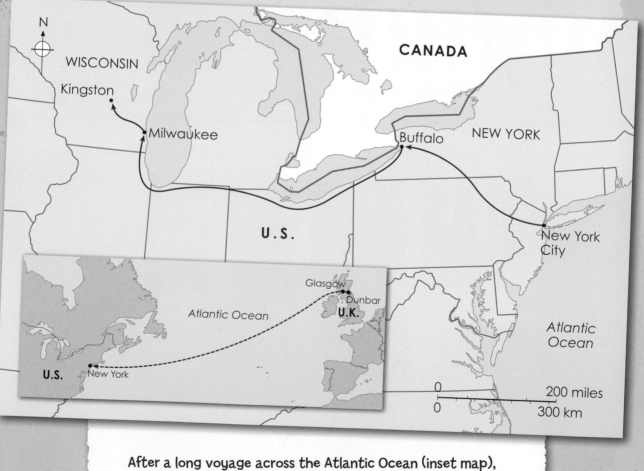

After a long voyage across the Atlantic Ocean (inset map),
John Muir and his family traveled more than 1,600 kilometers
(1,000 miles) to the middle of Wisconsin (main map).

John Muir loved to draw. When he was a boy, he sketched this picture of his home in Wisconsin.

Hard work

As the oldest boy, John was expected to help build the family home and plow the fields. It was hard work for an 11-year-old boy. John's father was strict. He made sure his boys completed their work.

John still found time to wander in the woods and fields near his home. He was delighted by all the new birds and other wildlife he discovered.

Learning from the frogs

John spent hours discovering the wildlife in the lake near his home. He studied the birds, fish, snakes, bees, and water bugs. When his father gave them some wood, John and his brothers quickly built a boat.

John wanted to learn to swim. His father told him, "Go to the frogs, and they will give you all the lessons you need." By watching the frogs, the boys learned how to dive and surface, and how to use their arms and legs.

John Muir's ideas led the U.S. government to create the national park system. These giant redwood sequoia trees are in woods named after him in the state of California.

The long walk

When he grew up, John worked in a factory. One day, a tool cut his eye. The accident nearly left him completely blind. When he recovered, he knew he had to follow his own path through life. He walked from Indiana to Florida (from the northern United States to the South) in just under two months. The walk covered 1,600 kilometers (1,000 miles). He later made his home in California.

Yosemite National Park, in California, is known for its glaciers, waterfalls, and beautiful valleys.

John Muir

John Muir's love of nature never left him. As an adult, he played a part in **preserving**, or saving, many beautiful places. He pushed to create Yosemite National Park, and he helped **found** the Sierra Club. This organization still works to preserve the environment today.

To America!

Lee begged his parents to let him go to America, and finally his father gave his blessing. He gave Lee $100. Lee traveled to Hong Kong with five other boys from his village. There, he bought a **steerage** ticket on a ship sailing east. Steerage was the cheapest ticket.

Many immigrants came to the United States in steerage. The journey was uncomfortable, but the tickets were cheap.

The trip was both exciting and confusing for Lee. His grandfather had told him stories about wizards in the United States and their evil ways. Now Lee was afraid to eat their food. Finally, the ship landed in San Francisco, California. Lee found a place to live in the Chinese part of the city. There he could get a decent meal.

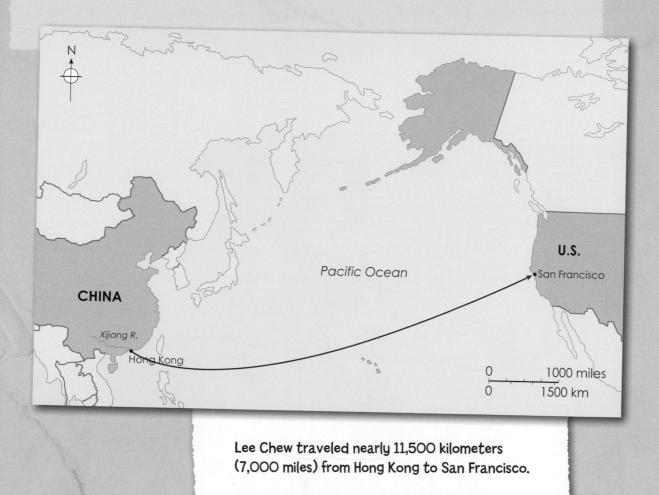

Lee Chew traveled nearly 11,500 kilometers (7,000 miles) from Hong Kong to San Francisco.

NUMBER CRUNCHING

In 1880 there were more than 100,000 Chinese men living in the United States, but fewer than 5,000 Chinese women. Like Lee Chew, many young men came to the United States on their own and sent money home to their families.

Working for a living

A man in the Chinese **quarter**, or neighborhood, got Lee a job working as a servant. He could not speak English, and he did not know anything about housework. The mother of the family he worked for showed Lee how to cook and clean. Lee got along well with the family. He was paid $3.50 a week. That's about $75 today.

Many Chinese people were forced to live in separate neighborhoods from white people.

After around two years as a servant, Lee had saved $400. He opened a **laundry**, which is a business that washes clothes. Many Chinese people owned laundries, because other jobs were not open to them. Lee later wrote that there are no laundries in China. Everything he knew about cleaning clothes, he learned in the United States.

Lee eventually moved to New York, where he opened a store. Years later, he wrote about his experiences in the United States.

Some Chinese people ran stores like this one.

HELPING HAND

Many white people felt that the Chinese were taking their jobs. In 1882 Chinese people were no longer allowed into the United States. Today, other groups have trouble immigrating there. The National Council of La Raza and the Central American Resource Center helps Mexican immigrants with legal, work, and rights issues.

Italy: 1894

In the mid-1800s, most immigrants came from northern European countries, such as Germany and Norway. By the end of the century, more people from Russia, eastern Europe, Greece, and Italy were coming to the United States. They often had a difficult life.

Garibaldi LaPolla was born in 1888 in a small town in southern Italy. When he was still very young, his father left Italy for the United States. He was not alone. More people from Italy have migrated to the United States than from any other country.

This is what Garibaldi's hometown of Rapolla looks like today.

In 1894, when Garibaldi was six years old, his father sent for the rest of the family. They journeyed across the ocean to New York. Once in the United States, they took a train to Montreal, in Canada. This is where Garibaldi's father was living.

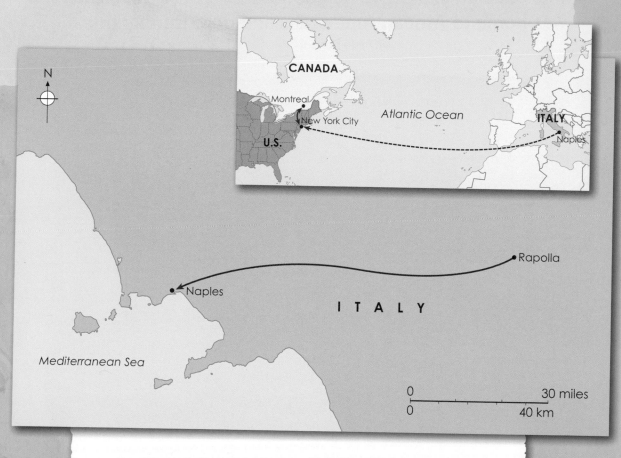

Garibaldi's family went from Rapolla to Naples (main map). From there they sailed to New York City and then traveled north to meet Garibaldi's father (inset map).

DAILY LIFE

Young Garibaldi LaPolla learned to love food and cooking from his father. He would help out at the bakery and watch his father in the kitchen. Many years later, he wrote a cookbook. It was called *Italian Cooking in the American Kitchen*.

Glossary

emigrant person who leaves his or her country to live in another one

feast large meal, usually for a special occasion

federal government government of a whole country. The federal government of the United States is based in Washington, D.C.

found create an organization. John Muir founded the Sierra Club.

immigrant person who used to live in another country

laundry business that washes clothes. Some hotels send their sheets and towels to laundries to be cleaned.

longshoreman person who loads and unloads ships

Midwest central part of the United States. The states of Illinois, Iowa, Wisconsin, and Indiana are all in the Midwest.

migrate leave one's home to live somewhere else

preserve keep something from being destroyed. John Muir wanted to preserve the natural beauty of the United States.

processed cleared for immigration. At Ellis Island, processing sometimes included a medical exam.

public school school funded by the government. Children do not need to pay to go to public schools.

quarter neighborhood where one kind of people lives

steerage cheapest kind of travel on a ship. Steerage passengers travel at the bottom of the boat.

tenement crowded block of apartments, usually in a poor neighborhood. Tenements were often very run down.

yearn want something badly. You may yearn for a new bicycle for your birthday.

Find Out More

Books

Cohen, Marina. *Changing Cultural Landscapes: How Are People and Their Communities Affected by Migration and Settlement?* (Investigating Human Migration and Settlement). New York: Crabtree, 2010.

Moreno, Barry. *Children of Ellis Island* (Images of America). Charleston, S.C.: Arcadia, 2005.

Spilsbury, Louise. *Moving People: Migration and Settlement* (Geography Focus). Chicago: Raintree, 2006.

Yep, Laurence, and Kathleen S. Yep. *The Dragon's Child: A Story of Angel Island.* New York: HarperCollins, 2008.

Websites

tenement.org/foreal
This is a web comic about the experiences of three recent immigrants to the United States.

www.ellisisland.org
This site includes information about the history of Ellis Island. It is also possible to do a search for passengers on ships that landed there.

www.unionsettlement.org/history
At the bottom of this page there is a video showing a brief history of the Union Settlement Association.

Places to visit

Tenement Museum
108 Orchard Street
New York, New York 10002
Tel: (212) 982-8420
Visit a restored tenement building on the Lower East Side of New York City, with guided tours for different grade levels.

Jane Addams Hull-House Museum
800 S. Halsted Street
Chicago, Illinois 60607
Tel: (312) 413-5353
Visit Hull House, one of the first settlement houses in the United States.

Index

OCT 2012

0 00 06 04049676

What's for lunch?

Bread

© 1999 by Franklin Watts
96 Leonard Street
London
EC2A 4XD

First American edition 1999 by Franklin Watts/Children's Press
A Division of Grolier Publishing
90 Sherman Turnpike
Danbury, CT 06816

Editor: Samantha Armstrong
Series Designer: Kirstie Billingham
Designer: Jason Anscomb
Consultants: Federation of Bakers; Flour Advisory Board
Reading Consultant: Prue Goodwin, Reading and Language
Information Centre, Reading.

ISBN 0-516-21546-9

A catalog record for this book is available from the Library of Congress

Visit Franklin Watts/Children's Press on the Internet at:
http://publishing.grolier.com

Printed in Hong Kong

What's for lunch?

Bread

Claire Llewellyn

CHILDREN'S PRESS®

A Division of Grolier Publishing

NEW YORK • LONDON • HONG KONG • SYDNEY
DANBURY, CONNECTICUT

Today we are having bread for lunch.
Bread is full of **fiber, protein, minerals,** and **vitamins.**
Eating bread gives us **energy.**

Bread is made mainly from **flour.**
Most of the bread we eat is made
from wheat flour. Wheat is grown
all over the world.

The young wheat plants grow green leaves and a tall stem. At the top of each stem is an **ear.** Tiny flowers grow on the ear. Later these flowers turn into **grains.**
It is the grains that are used to make flour.

Sometimes bread is made in a special shape, such as this wheatsheaf, to celebrate a festival.

Farmers check to see when the grain is dry and ready for storing. It is then kept in huge containers called **silos.** Some grain is saved for next year's seed. The grain that will be made into flour is sold to **flour millers.**

At the flour mill, the grains are crushed by rollers until they split into three different parts. Each part is **sifted** until it is a very fine flour.

The miller mixes the parts of the crushed grain together to make different kinds of flour. The miller also adds vitamins and minerals to the flour.
It is then ready to be sold to make bread.

Other **ingredients** are needed to make bread.
These are water, salt, and **yeast.**
They are mixed with the flour until it makes
a stretchy **dough.**
Then the dough is pressed, or **kneaded.**
The yeast makes the dough **rise.**

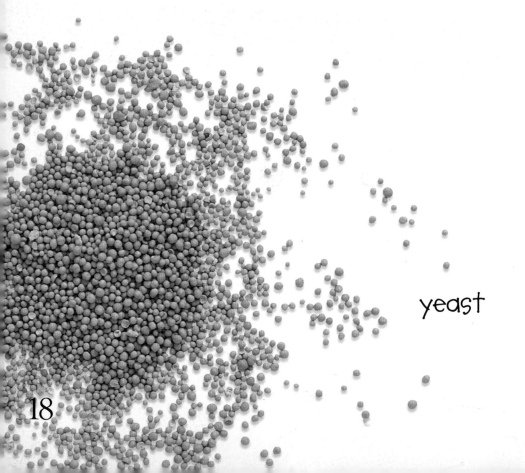

yeast

The dough is now divided into loaf shapes or put into pans. Then it is left to rise. After an hour, the dough is twice its original size. This is called **proving.** It is now ready to be baked in a huge oven.

After about twenty minutes, the loaves of bread are taken out of the oven and turned out of their pans. The bread cools down as it goes along a conveyor belt.

Most of the bread we eat is sliced and packed into plastic bags.
Wrapping the bread helps keep it fresh.
It is then taken to supermarkets to be sold.

Different types of bread are eaten all over the world. Ciabatta has olive oil added to it.

Bagels are chewy doughnut-shaped breads. Pita bread is flat because it has no yeast in it. Croissants are sweet and buttery.

Bread is delicious when it is still warm
from the oven.

It is a food that we eat every day.
It is filling, tasty, and good for us.

Glossary

combine harvester machine that harvests wheat and separates the grains from the stalks

disease something that attacks plants and animals

dough the mixture that is baked and becomes bread

ear of wheat the top part of the stalk where the grains grow

energy the strength to work and play

fiber something found in some foods which helps us to digest what we eat

flour the fine powder made from crushed wheat grains and which we use to make bread

flour millers people who make flour

grains the seeds of the wheat plant

harvest to take the crop from the field

ingredients the different parts needed to make something

kneaded	mixed and pressed by machine or by hand
minerals	materials found in rocks and also in our food. Minerals help us stay healthy
protein	something found in food that builds our bodies
proving	leaving the dough so that it can rise
to rise	when the dough puffs up because of the yeast and becomes light and airy
sifted	when something is put through a sieve to make it fine and powdery
silos	huge storage containers for grain
vitamins	something found in food that keeps us healthy
yeast	something added to bread dough to make it rise

Index

Picture credits: Holt Studios International: 6-7 (Willem Harinck), 8 (Nigel Cattlin), 10, 13 (Inga Spence), 15 (Willem Harinck), 19 (Nigel Cattlin); Federation of Bakers 20, 23, 24 (Tony Ross); Steve Shott: cover, backcover; All other photographs Tim Ridley, Wells Street Studios, London.
With thanks to Charlotte Trundley, Nyran Sri-Pathmanathan and Alex Wright.